Chronological Timeline of Psychology Development

(1832 – 2009)

By

Suripeddi Koundinya

M.A. Psychology
M.A. Astrology
M.Tech. Biotechnology

<u>Author Works</u>

Research Methods in Psychology (2022 JUNE)

Advanced Social Psychology (2022 JAN)

Cognitive, Life Span and Personality theories

[3 in1] (2021 MAY)

Formulae in Psychological Statistics (2020

MAY)

First Publication: 2022 JULY

Topics

Historical timeline
Chronology view
Types in Psychology

Suripeddi Koundinya is a certified Counseling Psychologist since 2020. He completed Masters (M.A) in Psychology from IGNOU. He further planning to do M.Phil. / Ph.D. in Psychology. He has an experience of doing consultation of Clients ranging from Children to Adults, dealing with ADHD, Anxiety, Sexual obsession, Dementia, Alcohol addicts, Marriage problems, Educational stress in Students, Suicidal tendencies, etc.

Follow Blog: https://psychologistera.blogspot.com/

<u>Historical timeline</u>

'Psychology' literally means 'science of the mind' (*psycho* meaning 'mind', or 'mental', and *-logy* meaning 'science').

In a very real sense, psychology is probably as old as humanity. In fact, some scientists have argued that one of the defining characteristics of human beings is the ability to study the behavior of others, imagine oneself in their positions and make predictions about their future behavior based on these insights.

Psychology is often defined as 'the science of behaviour'. Certainly, psychologists invest a considerable amount of time and effort in observing and measuring behaviour. But they are also interested in what people say about their experiences. Rather than studying a person's behaviour in isolation, they use the behaviour to find out about mental and biological processes, motives and personality traits. Therefore a definition of psychology as 'the science of behaviour' is inadequate.

Psychology as a field of experimental study **began in 1854 in Leipzig, Germany** when Gustav Fechner created the first theory of how judgments about sensory experiences are made and how to experiment on them.

The scientific study of psychology is a much more recent development, however. Many historians date the birth of modern psychology from the founding of the first experimental psychology laboratory by **Wilhelm Wundt in 1879**.

G. Stanley Hall, a student of Wilhelm Wundt, establishes first U.S. experimental psychology laboratory in 1883 at Johns Hopkins University.

The first doctorate in psychology is given to Joseph Jastrow, a student of G. Stanley Hall at Johns Hopkins University in 1886. Jastrow later becomes professor of psychology at the University of Wisconsin and serves as president of the American Psychological Association in 1900.

The academic title "professor of psychology" is given to James McKeen Cattell in 1888, the first use of this designation in the United States. A student of Wilhelm Wundt's, Cattell serves as professor of psychology at University of Pennsylvania and Columbia University.

G. Stanley Hall founds the American Psychological Association (APA) and serves as its first president. He later establishes two key journals in the field: American Journal of Psychology (1887) and Journal of Applied Psychology (1917).

Functionalism, an early school of psychology, focuses on the acts and functions of the mind rather than its internal contents. Its most prominent American advocates are William James and John Dewey, whose 1896 article "The Reflex Arc Concept in Psychology" promotes functionalism.

The founder of psychoanalysis, Sigmund Freud, introduces the term in a scholarly paper. Freud's psychoanalytic approach asserts that people are motivated by powerful, unconscious drives and conflicts. He develops an influential therapy based on this assertion, using free association and dream analysis.

Sigmund Freud introduces his theory of psychoanalysis in *The Interpretation of Dreams (1900)*, the first of 24 books he would write exploring such topics as the unconscious, techniques of free association, and sexuality as a driving force in human psychology.

Edward B. Titchener, a leading proponent of structuralism, publishes his Outline of Psychology. Structuralism is the view that all mental experience can be understood as a combination of simple elements or events. This approach focuses on the contents of the mind, contrasting with functionalism.

Lightner Witmer opens world's first psychological clinic to patients a laboratory at University of Pennsylvania in 1896, shifting his focus from experimental work to practical application of his findings.

Using standardized tests, Alfred Binet and Theodore Simon develop a scale of general intelligence on the basis of mental age (1905). Later researchers refine this work into the concept of intelligence quotient; IQ, mental age over physical age. From their beginning, such tests' accuracy and fairness are challenged.

John B. Watson publishes "Psychology as Behavior," launching behaviorism in 1913. In contrast to psychoanalysis, behaviorism focuses on observable and measurable behavior.

Francis Cecil Sumner earns a **First African American doctorate** Ph.D. in psychology in 1920 under G. Stanley Hall at Clark University. Sumner later serves as chair of the Howard University psychology department.

Swiss psychologist Jean Piaget publishes *The Child's Conception of the World (1920)*, prompting the study of cognition in the developing child.

Swiss psychiatrist Hermann Rorschach devises a personality test (1921) based on patients' interpretations of inkblots.

Charles Frederick Menninger and his sons Karl Augustus and William Clair found The Menninger Clinic in 1925 at Topeka, Kansas. They take a compassionate approach to the treatment of mental illness, emphasizing both psychological and psychiatric disciplines. **Menninger Clinic founded** First Nobel Prize for psychological research in 1927.

Psychiatrist Hans Berger invents the electroencephalogram in 1929 and tests it on his son. The device graphs the electrical activity of the brain by means of electrodes attached to the head.

Alcoholics Anonymous (AA) is founded by Bob Smith of Akron, Ohio in 1935. AA's group meetings format and 12-step program becomes the model for many other mutual-support therapeutic groups.

Kurt Koffka, a founder of the movement, publishes Principles of Gestalt Psychology in 1935. Gestalt (German for "whole" or "essence") psychology asserts that psychological phenomena must be viewed not as individual elements but as a coherent whole.

Walter Freeman performs first frontal lobotomy in the United States in 1936 at George Washington University in Washington, D.C. By 1951, more than 18,000 such operations have been performed. The procedure, intended to relieve severe and debilitating psychosis, is controversial.

Psychologist Karen Horney publishes *The Neurotic Personality of Our Time in 1937*. Horney goes on to challenge many of Freud's theories, as have many later psychologists and scholars. Specifically, she questions Freud's theories on the Oedipal Complex and castration anxiety.

B.F. Skinner publishes *The Behavior of Organisms*, introducing the concept of operant conditioning in 1938. The work draws widespread attention to behaviorism and inspires laboratory research on conditioning.

Anna Freud publishes The Psychoanalytic Treatment of Children in 1946, introducing basic concepts in the theory and practice of child psychoanalysis.

U.S. President Harry Truman signs the National Mental Health Act in 1946, providing generous funding for psychiatric education and research for the first time in U.S. history. This act leads to the creation in 1949 of the National Institute of Mental Health (NIMH).

In 1951, Studies are published reporting that the drug imipramine may be able to lessen depression. Eight years later, the FDA approves its use in the United States under the name Tofranil.

The anti-psychotic drug chlorpromazine (known as Thorazine) is tested on a patient in a Paris military hospital in 1952. Approved for use in the United States in 1954, it becomes widely prescribed.

The American Psychological Association publishes the first edition of *Ethical Standards of Psychologists in 1953*. The document undergoes continuous review and is now known as APA's Ethical Principles of Psychologists and Code of Conduct.

Social Psychologist Gordon Allport publishes *The Nature of Prejudice in 1954*, which draws on various approaches in psychology to examine prejudice through different lenses. It is widely read by the general public and influential in establishing psychology's usefulness in understanding social issues.

In his studies of epilepsy in 1954, neuroscientist Wilder G. Penfield begins to uncover the relationship between chemical activity in the brain and psychological phenomena. His findings set the stage for widespread research on the biological role in psychological phenomena.

The development of psychoactive drugs in the 1950s and their approval by the FDA initiates a new form of treatment for mental illness. Among the first such drugs is Doriden, also known as Rorer, an anti-anxiety medication approved in 1954.

In the wake of psychoanalysis and behaviorism, humanistic psychology emerges as the "third force" in psychology led by Carl Rogers and Abraham Maslow, who publishes Motivation and Personality in 1954, this approach centers on the conscious mind, free will, human dignity, and the capacity for self-actualization.

Inspired by work in mathematics and other disciplines, psychologists begin to focus on cognitive states and processes. George A. Miller's 1956 article "The Magical Number Seven, Plus or Minus Two" on information processing is an early application of the cognitive approach.

Noam Chomsky publishes *Syntactic Structures in 1957*, marking a major advancement in the study of linguistics. The book helps spawn the field of psycholinguistics, the psychology of language.

The FDA approves the use of chlordiazepoxide (known as Librium) for treatment of non-psychotic anxiety in 1960. A similar drug, diazepam (Valium), is approved in 1963.

In 1963, U.S. President John F. Kennedy calls for and later signs the Community Mental Health

Centers Act, which mandates the construction of community facilities instead of large, regional mental hospitals. Congress ends support for the program in 1981, reducing overall funds and folding them into a mental health block-grant program.

Neal E. Miller receives the National Medal of Science in 1964, the highest scientific honor given in the United States, for his studies of motivation and learning. He is the first psychologist to be awarded this honor.

The FDA approves lithium carbonate in 1964 to treat patients with bipolar mood disorders. It is marketed under the trade names Eskalith, Lithonate, and Lithane.

After intense debate, the American Psychiatric Association removes homosexuality from the Diagnostic and Statistical Manual of Mental Disorders (DSM) in 1973. The widely used reference manual is revised to state that sexual orientation "does not necessarily constitute a psychiatric disorder."

A new brain scanning technique, Positron Emission Tomography (PET) in 1974, is tested. By tracing chemical markers, PET maps brain function in more detail than earlier techniques.

Richard Dawkins publishes The Selfish Gene in 1976, which begins to popularize the idea of evolutionary psychology. This approach applies principles from evolutionary biology to the structure and function of the human brain. It offers new ways of looking at social phenomena such as aggression and sexual behavior.

The U.S. District Court finds the use of standardized IQ tests in 1979 at California public schools illegal. The decision in the case, Larry P. v. Wilson Riles, upholds the plaintiff's position that the tests discriminate against African American students.

In 1981, the epidemic of acquired immunodeficiency syndrome (AIDS) and human immunodeficiency virus (HIV) infection presents mental health professionals with challenges ranging from at-risk patients' anxiety and depression to AIDS-related dementia.

In Acts of Meaning, Four Lectures on Mind and Culture, Jerome Bruner helps formulate cultural psychology in 1990, an approach drawing on philosophy, linguistics, and anthropology. Refined and expanded by Hazel Markus and other researchers, cultural psychology focuses on the influences and relationship among mind, cultural community and behavior.

In 2000, sixteen public research institutions around the world complete a "working draft" mapping of the human genetic code, providing a research basis for a new understanding of human development and disease. A similar, privately funded, project is currently underway.

<u>Chronology view</u>

1832: Wilhelm Wundt born in Neckarau, Baden, Germany, outside of Leipzig, on August 16.

1849: Ivan Pavlov born in the village of Ryazan, Russia.

1856: Sigismund Freud is born (changes his name to Sigmund at age 22).

1857: Alfred Binet born on July 8 in Nice, France.

1857: Louis Pasteur introduces his germ theory of fermentation.

1857: Wilhelm Wundt begins a seven-year position as lecturer in physiology at Heidelberg. During this time he serves as an assistant Hermann von Helmholtz.

1859: Charles Darwin presents his theory of evolution in On the Origin of Species.

1864: Wilhelm Wundt appointed associate professor in physiology at University of Heidelberg.

1873: Sigmund Freud receives a summa cum laude award on graduation from the Gymnasium. He is already able to read in several languages.

1873–74: Wilhelm Wundt publishes first edition of Principles of Psychology.

1875: Carl Jung born in a country parsonage at Kesswil in Canton Thurgau, Switzerland.

1875: Wilhelm Wundt appointed one of two fellow professors at Leipzig University, focusing on practical-scientific theories.

1876: Robert Yerkes born on May 26 in Breadysville, Pennsylvania.

1876: Alexander Graham Bell patents the telephone. 1877: Sigmund Freud joins Brücke's laboratory.

1878: Alfred Binet receives a license in law, a career he chose not to pursue.

1879: Ivan Pavlov graduates from the Medical Academy; wins a gold medal in student competition.

1879: Wilhelm Wundt established the first laboratory for experimental psychology.

1880: Max Wertheimer born on April 15, 1880, in Prague.

1880: Alfred Binet publishes his first article, "On the Fusion of Similar Sensations."

1881: Sigmund Freud awarded a delayed doctor's degree in medicine.

1883–84: Wilhelm Wundt's laboratory receives official status at Leipzig as an institution of its department of philosophy.

1884: Francis Galton sets up a laboratory in London to measure individual differences in mental abilities.

1884: Sigmund Freud discovers the analgesic properties of cocaine.

1885: Karen Horney is born outside Hamburg, Germany. 1886: Alfred Binet publishes his first book, The Psychology of Reasoning. 1886: Sigmund Freud starts private practice.

1887: Sigmund Freud starts using hypnosis.

1890: Kurt Lewin born in Germany, now a part of Poland.

1890: James McKeen Cattell publishes a paper in which he coined the term "mental test."

1894: Alfred Binet receives a doctoral degree in natural science from the Sorbonne.

1895: Alfred Binet helps found the first French psychological journal.

1896: Sigmund Freud for the first time uses the term "psychoanalysis."

1896: Wilhelm Wundt dies in Groábothen, German, near Leipzig, August 31. His book, Outlines of Psychology, was published the same year.

1896: Alfred Binet publishes a paper outlining "individual psychology" with Victor Henri.

1896: Jean Piaget born in Neuchatel, Switzerland.

1897: Ivan Pavlov publishes "Lectures on the Work of the Main Digestive Glands."

1897: Sigmund Freud postulates Oedipus complex.

1899: Alfred Binet began working with Théodore Simon. 1899: Sigmund Freud's The Interpretation of Dreams is published on November 4.

1900: After finishing medical school at the University of Basel, Carl Jung travels to Zurich to study psychiatry under Eugen Bleuler, a worldfamous expert on schizophrenia.

1900: Gregor Mendel's basic laws of heredity, which went unnoticed when first set forth in the 1860s, are rediscovered.

1900–09: Carl Jung works as a psychiatric resident at the Burghölzli, a famous mental hospital in Zurich. 1900–20: Wilhelm Wundt's Volkerpsychologie (Folk Psychology) published in 10 volumes.

1902: Robert Yerkes receives a PhD in psychology from Harvard and begins teaching comparative psychology at Harvard.

1902: Sigmund Freud begins the Wednesday Psychological Society meetings at his home.

1902: Carl Rogers is born in Oak Park, Illinois.

1904: Max Wertheimer receives his doctorate in philosophy at the University of Würzburg.

1904: Ivan Pavlov awarded the Nobel Prize in Physiology or Medicine.

1904: B.F. Skinner born March 20.

1905: George Alexander Kelly born on a farm near Perth, Kansas.

1905: Alfred Binet, along with Theodore Simon, introduces the first version of the Binet-Simon Scale.

1905: Albert Einstein publishes his special theory of relativity.

1906: Carl Jung publishes a book on schizophrenia that applies Sigmund Freud's psychoanalytic approach to the study of psychosis.

1906: Carl Jung starts his correspondence with Sigmund Freud.

1906: Jean Piaget publishes first article in local journal.

1908: Anne Anastasi born on December 19 in New York City.

1908: Robert Yerkes publishes the Yerkes-Dodson law, developed with John Dodson, which related the strength of a stimulus to the speed of avoidance learning.

1908: Abraham Maslow born in Manhattan.

1909: Publication of Sigmund Freud's Analysis of a Phobia in a Five-Year-Old Boy (Little Hans).

1909: Carl Jung travels with Sigmund Freud to the United States to give lectures at Clark University in Massachusetts.

1910: Max Wertheimer discovers the phi phenomenon on a train ride and published his groundbreaking paper "Experimental Studies of the Perception of Movement" two years later.

1910: Construction of Ivan Pavlov's "Towers of Silence" begins.

1911: Robert Yerkes founds the Journal of Animal Behavior, the first U.S. scientific journal devoted solely to animal behavior research.

1911: Alfred Binet makes the last revision of the Binet-Simon Scale. Dies on October 18.

1913: Mary Salter (later Ainsworth) born in Glendale, Ohio.

1913: Carl Jung breaks with Sigmund Freud. Publishes Psychology of the Unconscious, the first account of his analytical psychology as an approach to therapy distinct from psychoanalysis.

1913–14: Carl Jung experiences a midlife crisis or period of psychological turmoil that resolves with the outbreak of World War I in July 1914.

1913–17: Robert Yerkes works half-time as a psychologist in the Psychopathic Department at Boston State Hospital.

1914: Kenneth Bancroft Clark born in Panama.

1914: Kurt Lewin volunteers to serve in World War.

1915: Robert Yerkes introduces a point scale for measuring intelligence, developed with J. W. Bridges.

1916 -The first psychology department and first psychology laboratory in India was established in

1916 under the leadership of **Dr. N.N Sen Gupta** (Dalal A. K & Misra A., 2010) at Calcutta University. He was a Hardward educated Indian psychologist, Philosopher and professor. He, along with Gunamudian Davi Boaz, is known as the founder of modern psychology in India.

1916: Lewis Terman introduced the Stanford-Binet Intelligence Scales, a U.S. version of the BinetSimon Scale that modified it substantially.

1917: Kurt Lewin wounded in war.

1917: Robert Yerkes elected president of the American Psychological Association and later becomes a member of the National Research Council.

1917–18: Robert Yerkes chairs a committee that developed the U.S. Army Alpha and Beta intelligence tests during World War I.

1918: Jean Piaget receives PhD in Natural Sciences, University of Neuchatel. He works in Eugen Bleuler's psychiatric clinic at the University of Zurich and develops his technique of the clinical interview.

1919: Kenneth Bancroft Clark comes to America with mother and sister.

1919–24: Robert Yerkes works for the National Research Council.

1920: Sigmund Freud publishes Beyond the Pleasure Principle.

1920: Wilhelm Wundt publishes autobiography entitled Erlebtes und Erkanntes.

1921: Sigmund Freud publishes Group Psychology and the Analysis of the Ego.

1921: Aaron Temkin Beck born in Providence, Rhode Island.

1921: Carl Jung publishes Psychological Types, a major work that secures his reputation as an original thinker.

1921: Jean Piaget appointed research director of the Institut Jean-Jacques Rousseau in Geneva, and publishes article in the Archives de Psychologie stating that logic is not innate but develops over time through interactive processes of self-regulation.

1922: Dr. Girindra Shekar Bose, who succeeded Dr. N.N Sengupta at Calcutta University established the Indian Psychoanalytical Society, by his intimate contact and support of Sigmund Freud. It is affiliated to the international psychoanalytic Association (Jain, 2005) (Dalal, 2011). Girindra Shekar Bose has the appreciation as the first PhD scholar from Indian psychological field. He received his PhD from Calcutta on the 'concept of repression'.

1923: Jean Piaget publishes The Language and Thought of the Child. Four more books follow, bringing him worldwide fame before the age of 30.

1923: Sigmund Freud diagnosed with cancer of the jaw. Publication of The Ego and the Id.

1924–44: Robert Yerkes holds a post as professor of psychobiology at Yale University.

1924: The second oldest Department of psychology established at the University of Mysore in India, headed by M. V Gopalaswamy. The department was offering M.A Degree in psychology until 1998. From 1998 syllabus revision has took place and the degree offered as M.Sc in psychology (Dalal A. K & Misra A., 2010).

1925: The **first Indian Psychological Association** established by the constant effort of S.N Gupta (Jain, 2005).

1925: Jean Piaget begins the study of the intellectual development of his three children from infancy through their teenage years.

1925: Albert Bandura born on December 4, 1925, in Mundare, Alberta, Canada.

1926- The Indian journal of psychology is founded and the first official founding editor was N.N Sen Gupta (Jain, 2005).

1926: Carl Brigham introduced the forerunner of the SAT.

1927: Lawrence Kohlberg born in Bronxville, New York.

1927: Ivan Pavlov publishes "Lectures on the Work of the Large Hemispheres of the Brain."

1928: Albert Einstein and Jean Piaget meet. Einstein suggests that Piaget study the origins in children of the notions of time and simultaneity.

1929: N.N Sen Gupta, along with Radhakamal Mukerjee published instruction to social psychology which named the first text covering the topic of social psychology published in India. In the same year when Sen Gupta appointed as the professor of Philosophy at the University of Lucknow, he introduced psychology into the philosophy curricula. It prepared the ground to establish Department of Experimental psychology at the University of Lucknow (Dalal, 2011).

1929: Robert Yerkes publishes The Great Apes: A Study of Anthropoid Life, co-authored with his wife, Ada Watterson Yerkes.

1929: Jean Piaget teaches the history of scientific thought at the University of Geneva until 1939. Begins 35-year tenure as director of the International Bureau of Education in Geneva.

1929–41: Robert Yerkes founds and directs the Yale Laboratories of Primate Biology, the first laboratory for nonhuman primate research in the United States.

1930: Anne Anastasi awarded a PhD from Columbia University. Hired as instructor of psychology at Barnard College.

1930: B.F. Skinner initiates research in reflexes.

1931: George Alexander Kelly receives his PhD from the University of Iowa.

1931–34: Abraham Maslow conducts primate research with Harry Harlow and completes a master's thesis and doctoral dissertation on primate behavior.

1932: Karen Horney moves to United States.

1933: Kurt Lewin moves to United States to escape the rise of Hitler.

1933: Sigmund Freud has a letter exchange with Albert Einstein on the topic Why the War? The Nazis publicly burn Freud's work in Berlin.

1933: Adolf Hitler became dictator of Germany.

1934: Max Wertheimer arrives in New York and begins teaching at the "University in Exile" for the next 10 years.

1934: Kenneth Bancroft Clark earns his bachelor's degree from Howard University. Gains his master's the following year.

1934: Karen Horney takes teaching position at Washington-Baltimore Society for Psychoanalysis.

1935–37: Abraham Maslow completes postdoctoral fellowship at Columbia University. Research on sexuality and dominance in humans.

1936: Ivan Pavlov dies on February 27 after developing pneumonia at the age of 86.

1936: Karen Horney publishes Feminine Psychology.

1936: Jean Piaget publishes The Origins of Intelligence in Children based on his observations of his three children.

1937: Carl Jung invited by Yale University to deliver the Terry Lectures on psychology and religion.

1937: Anne Anastasi publishes her first major work, Differential Psychology, through Macmillan Publishing, New York.

1937–51: Abraham Maslow obtains a faculty position at Brooklyn College. Eventually reaches rank of associate professor.

1937–61: Carl Jung continues to practice medicine in Küssnacht, a suburb of Zurich, until his death in 1961.

1938: March 13th: Austria is annexed by Germany. Sigmund Freud's house and the headquarters of the Vienna Association of Psychoanalysis are searched. Anna Freud is arrested and interrogated by the Gestapo. In June, Freud and his family immigrate to Great Britain.

1938: B.F. Skinner's The Behavior of Organisms published.

1939: Mary Salter Ainsworth receives her PhD from the University of Toronto.

1939: Sigmund Freud dies. Moses and Monotheism is published.

1939: David Wechsler published the Wechsler Bellevue Scale, an adult-oriented intelligence test.

1939: Anne Anastasi appointed assistant professor of psychology and department chair, Queens College of the City University of New York.

1940: Jean Piaget appointed Chair of Experimental Psychology, University of Geneva (until 1971).

1940: Carl Rogers receives a full professorship at Ohio State University.

1941–45: George Alexander Kelly serves during World War II as a Navy aviation psychologist, and teaches at the University of Maryland.

1942: B.F. Skinner awarded the Warren Medal by the Society of Experimental Psychologists.

1942: Jean Piaget lectures at the College of France during Nazi occupation. Lectures compiled into The Psychology of Intelligence published in 1963.

1942: Karen Horney publishes Self-Analysis.

1942: Mary D. Salter Ainsworth enters the Canadian Women's Army Corps.

1943: Max Wertheimer dies at his home after suffering a heart attack.

1944: Kurt Lewin invited to set up research institute at MIT.

1945: B.F. Skinner takes over the psychology department at the University of Indiana, where he developed the Teaching Machine and Aircrib.

1945: Mary D. Salter Ainsworth serves as Director of Women's Rehabilitation at Veteran Army Services Hospital.

1945: Carl Rogers joins faculty at the University of Chicago. Elected president of the American Psychological Association.

1945: Max Wertheimer publishes his only book, Productive Thinking.

1946: Aaron Temkin Beck graduates with a medical degree from Yale University.

1946: Mary D. Salter Ainsworth returns to University of Toronto to teach.

1946: George Alexander Kelly accepted the position as director of clinical programs for the school of psychology at the Ohio State University, following Carl Rogers.

1947: Kurt Lewin dies of heart attack.

1948: B.F. Skinner's Walden Two published. 1949: NATO is established.

1949: David Wechsler introduced the Wechsler Intelligence Scale for Children.

1949: Psychological research wing was established by India Government Defence Ministry with the aim of the inclusion of psychologists on research and selection boards (Jain, 2005).

1950: Kenneth Bancroft Clark publishes "Effect of Prejudice and Discrimination on Personality Development" for the Mid-Century White House Conference on Children and Youth.

1950: Mary D. Salter Ainsworth moves to London.

1950: Jean Piaget publishes his three volume book, Introduction a l'epistemologie genetique.

1951: Korean War breaks out. Aaron Temkin Beck takes a position at Valley Forge Field Hospital and treats soldiers with post-traumatic stress disorder.

1951–69: Abraham Maslow obtains a faculty position at Brandeis University. He serves as department chair until 1961.

1952: Albert Bandura receives a PhD in clinical psychology from the University of Iowa.

1952: Karen Horney dies of stomach cancer at age 67.

1953: Albert Bandura takes a job as a psychology instructor at Stanford University.

1953: DNA is discovered.

1954: The publication of Abraham Maslow's Motivation and Personality brings national prominence.

1954: Mary Salter Ainsworth moves to Africa; starts Uganda mother-infant studies.

1954: Brown v. Board of Education uses Kenneth Bancroft Clark's studies as a basis for school desegregation.

1954: Anne Anastasi publishes Psychological Testing, Macmillan, New York.

1954: Aaron Temkin Beck joins the Department of Psychiatry of the University of Pennsylvania. 1955: Mary Salter Ainsworth hired as lecturer at Johns Hopkins in Baltimore.

1955: W. W. Norton & Company publishes George Alexander Kelly's ground-breaking, two-volume work, The Psychology of Personal Constructs.

1955: Jean Piaget's International Center for Genetic Epistemology opens at the University of Geneva.

1955: First edition of Kenneth Bancroft Clark's book Prejudice and Your Child published as Clark's first public scientific commentary.

1956: Fixed interval schedule of reinforcement described by B.F. Skinner.

1956: Robert Yerkes dies on February 3.

1958: Lawrence Kohlberg graduates from University of Chicago with a doctoral degree.

1959: Albert Bandura publishes his first book, Adolescent Aggression, with Richard Walters.

1959: Kenneth Bancroft Clark elected president of the Society for the Psychological Study of Social Issues.

1961: The first issue of The Journal of Humanistic Psychology, founded by Abraham Maslow, is published.

1961: Kenneth Bancroft Clark awarded the Spingarn Medal by the NAACP.

1962: Abraham Maslow publishes Toward a Psychology of Being.

1962: Mary D. Salter Ainsworth begins Baltimore replication study of mother-infant dyads.

1962–63: Abraham Maslow consults with Andy Kay at Non-Linear Systems.

1963: Albert Bandura publishes Social Learning and Personality Development, which summarized his research on observational learning and the Bobo doll experiments.

1963: President John F. Kennedy is assassinated while riding in a motorcade through Dallas.

1964: Carl Rogers elected "Humanist of the Year" by the American Humanist Association.

1964: Albert Bandura becomes a full professor at Stanford.

1965: George Alexander Kelly begins research position at Brandeis University, where Abraham Maslow is also working at the time.

1965: Kenneth Bancroft Clark publishes Dark Ghetto. 1966: Abraham Maslow is elected president of the American Psychological Association.

1966: B.F. Skinner introduces the concept of critical period in reinforcing an event.

1966: Jean Piaget publishes The Psychology of the Child with Barbel Inhelder.

1967: George Alexander Kelly dies on March 6.

1967: Mary Salter Ainsworth publishes Infancy in Uganda.

1968: Lawrence Kohlberg becomes a full professor at Harvard University. Later founds the Center for Moral Development and Education there.

1968: B.F. Skinner identifies the critical characteristics of programmed instruction.

1969: Lawrence Kohlberg studies moral development in an Israeli kibbutz.

1969: Jean Piaget awarded distinguished Scientific Contribution Award by the American Psychological Association. He is the first European to receive the award.

1970: Carl Rogers' On Encounter Groups published. He would publish two more books before his death.

1970: Abraham Maslow dies of a heart attack at his home in Menlo Park, California.

1971: Lawrence Kohlberg co-authors "The Adolescent as Philosopher" with Carol Gilligan. Kohlberg also contracts a parasitic illness in Central America, which afflicts him for 16 years.

1971: Kenneth Bancroft Clark elected president of the American Psychological Association. Clark has been the only African American to serve in that capacity.

1971: B.F. Skinner publishes Beyond Freedom and Dignity.

1972: B.F. Skinner receives the Humanist of the Year Award by the American Humanist Association.

1974: Albert Bandura serves as president of the American Psychological Association.

1974: Aaron Temkin Beck publishes The Prediction of Suicide.

1975: Mary Salter Ainsworth leaves Johns Hopkins for University of Virginia.

1975–95: Kenneth Bancroft Clark serves on the New York Board of Regents.

1977: Albert Bandura publishes Social Learning Theory, which aroused interest in social learning and modelling. 1978: Mary D. Salter Ainsworth publishes Patterns of Attachment.

1979: Anne Anastasi named professor emeritus at Fordham.

1980: Jean Piaget dies at the age of 84 in Geneva, Switzerland.

1983: B.F. Skinner publishes Enjoying Old Age.

1984: The virus that causes AIDS is identified by two groups of scientists in France and the United States. 1984: Mary Salter Ainsworth retires from the University of Virginia as Professor Emeritus.

1985: Robert Sternberg presents his three-part theory of intelligence in Beyond IQ

1986: Albert Bandura publishes Social Foundations of Thought and Action: A Social Cognitive Theory, which described his social-cognitive theory of human functioning.

1986: Carl Rogers travels to Russia to facilitate conflict resolution.

1987: Carl Rogers dies of heart attack.

1987: Lawrence Kohlberg commits suicide by drowning in Winthrop, Massachusetts.

1988: Aaron Temkin Beck publishes Love is Never Enough.

1990: B.F. Skinner dies on August 18.

1994: Kenneth Bancroft Clark receives the APA Award for Outstanding Lifetime Contribution to Psychology.

1997: Albert Bandura publishes Self-Efficacy: The Exercise of Control, which set forth his ideas about self-efficacy beliefs.

1997- The first Asian conference Psychology was held in Singapore. It includes ten countries named Malaysia, Indonesia, Philippines, Hong Kong, Taiwan, India, Austria, New Zealand, Korea and Singapore and together formed the Asia Oceanic Psychological Association (Robert B. Lawson, Jean E.G, Kristian M. B, 2008).

1998: Mary Salter Ainsworth receives APA Gold Medal Award for Life Achievement in the Science of Psychology.

1999: Mary Salter Ainsworth dies in Charlottesville, Virginia.

2004: Aaron Temkin Beck publishes Cognitive Therapy of Personal Disorders, second edition.

2005- The Asian Applied psychology international regional conference was held in Bangkok, Thailand.

In the same year, Asian psychological association was also held in Jakarta, Indonesia (Robert B. Lawson, Jean E.G, Kristian M. B, 2008).

2009- Indian School Psychology Association established in 2009 to promote school psychology in India and Abroad by the guidance and headship of Prof. B. Mukhopadhyay. (Indian School Psychology Association | InSPA)

Types in Psychology

Here is a list of the many subfields of psychology:

Abnormal psychology: Nature and development of abnormal behaviour, thoughts, feelings associated with distress or impaired functioning that is not a culturally expected response to an event.

Behaviour genetics: Impact of heredity on animal and human behaviour.

Clinical psychology: Diagnosis, treatment, and prevention of mental disorders and disabilities.

Cognitive neuroscience: Neuronal basis of mental processes.

Cognitive psychology: Study of the processes by which sensory information is transformed, reduced, elaborated, stored, retrieved and used.

Community psychology: Person–environment interactions and the ways society impacts upon individual and community functioning. Focuses on social issues, social institutions, and other settings that influence individuals, groups, and organizations. Emphasizes changing social systems to prevent psychological problems.

Comparative psychology: The study of behaviour in different species.

Consumer psychology: The effects of advertising, marketing, packaging, and display on the behaviour of purchasers.

Counselling psychology: Traditionally associated with the field of education, counselling psychology may include vocational guidance as well as helping persons resolve problems or role issues related to work or school or family matters.

Cross-cultural psychology: Impact of culture on human behaviour.

Developmental psychology: Change in behavioural and mental processes over the life span.

Developmental psychopathology: The origins and course of individual patterns of behavioural maladaptation whatever the age of onset, causes or transformations in behavioural manifestation.

<u>Educational psychology</u> (also called school psychology): Diagnosis and treatment of educational, emotional, and behavioural problems in children and teenagers.

<u>Environmental psychology</u>: Relationships between human behaviour and the physical environment.

<u>Ergonomic psychology</u> (also called human factors and engineering psychology): Design of tasks, equipment, and work places to maximize performance and well-being and to minimize fatigue, boredom and accidents.

<u>Evolutionary psychology</u>: Applies an evolutionary perspective to understanding human behaviour and mental processes.

<u>Family psychology</u>: Study of the family as a system, and of relationships within the system.

<u>Forensic and criminological psychology</u>: Psychological aspects of legal processes and crimes.

<u>Health psychology</u>: Lifestyle and physical health, the identification of psychological causes and correlates of health and illness, psychological aspects of health promotion and the prevention and treatment of illness.

Mathematical/quantitativepsychology: Development of mathematical models of behaviour and derivation of statistical methods for analysing data collected by psychologists.

Medical psychology (also referred to as behavioural medicine): Psychological aspects of medical practice, the doctor–patient relationship, reactions to medical advice, improving treatment compliance. Psychological issues that arise in medical treatment of children and adolescents have given rise to the field of paediatric psychology.

Neuropsychology: Study of the impact of disorders of the nervous system (especially the brain) on behaviour.

Organizational psychology: Study of structures and functions of organizations and the activities of the people within them. Included in its remit are job satisfaction, employee attitudes and motivation, and their effects on absenteeism, labour turnover, and organizational productivity and efficiency.

<u>Personality psychology/Individual Differences</u>: Study of characteristics that make each person unique.

<u>Social psychology</u>: Investigation of the reciprocal influence of the individual and his or her social context.

<u>Sport/exercise psychology</u>: Reciprocal effects of psychological factors on sports/exercise.